NEWS OF THE HOUR

Mark's Gospel

by Peter Bolt

& Tony Payne

News of the Hour
© Peter Bolt & Tony Payne, 1997, 2000

Published in the UK by:
The Good Book Company
Elm House, 37 Elm Road
New Malden, Surrey KT3 3HB
Tel: 0845-225-0880
Fax: 0845-225-0990
Email: admin@thegoodbook.co.uk
website: www.thegoodbook.co.uk

ISBN 1-873166-60-5

Typesetting and design by Matthias Media.
Cover illustration by Richard Knight

Contents

How to make the most of these studies 5

1   At that time, Jesus 9

2   As one who had authority 19

3   This is what the kingdom will be like 27

4   The sheep and their shepherds 33

5   Who do you say I am? 41

6   What must I do? 47

7   He overturned the tables 55

8   When will these things happen? 63

9   The hour has come 73

10   He is not here 81

Tips for leaders 87

How to make the most of these studies

1. What is an interactive Bible study?

These 'interactive' Bible studies are a bit like a guided tour of a famous city. The studies will take you through Mark's Gospel, pointing out things along the way, filling in background details, and suggesting avenues for further exploration. But there is also time for you to do some sight-seeing of your own—to wander off, have a good look for yourself, and form your own conclusions.

In other words, we have designed these studies to fall half-way between a sermon and a set of unadorned Bible study questions. We want to provide stimulation and input and point you in the right direction, while leaving you to do a lot of the exploration and discovery yourself.

We hope that these studies will stimulate lots of 'interaction'—interaction with the Bible, with the things we've written, with your own current thoughts and attitudes, with other people as you discuss them, and with God as you talk to him about it all.

2. The format

Each study contains sections of text to introduce, summarize, suggest and provoke. We've left plenty of room in the margins for you to jot comments and questions as you read.

Interspersed throughout the teaching are three types of 'interaction', each with its own symbol:

For starters

Questions to help you think about society and your own experience, in a way that tunes you in to the issues being raised by the Bible passage.

Investigate

Questions to help you investigate key parts of the Bible.

Think it through

Questions to help you think through the implications of your discoveries and write down your own thoughts and reactions.

When you come to one of these symbols, you'll know that it's time to do some work of your own.

3. Suggestions for individual study

- Before you begin, pray that God would open your eyes to what he is saying in Mark's Gospel and give you the spiritual strength to do something about it. You may be spurred to pray again at the end of the study.
- Work through the study, following the directions as you go. Write in the spaces provided.
- Resist the temptation to skip over the *Think it through* sections. It is important to think about the sections of text (rather than just accepting them as true) and to ponder the implications for your life. Writing these things down is a very valuable way to get your thoughts working.
- Take what opportunities you can to talk to others about what you've learnt.

4. Suggestions for group study

- Much of the above applies to group study as well. The studies are suitable for structured Bible study or cell groups, as well as for more informal pairs and threesomes. Get together with a friend/s and work through them at your own pace. You don't need the formal structure of a 'group' to gain maximum benefit.
- It is *vital* that group members work through the study themselves *before* the group meets. The group discussion can take place comfortably in an hour (depending on how side-tracked you get!), but only if all the members have done the work and are familiar with the material.
- Spend most of the group time discussing the 'interactive' sections—*For starters, Investigate* and *Think it through.* Reading all the text together will take too long and should be unnecessary if the group members have done their preparation. You may wish to underline and read aloud particular paragraphs or sections of text that you think are important.
- The role of the group leader is to direct the course of the discussion and to try to draw the threads together at the end. This will mean a little extra preparation—underlining important sections of text to emphasize, working out which questions are worth concentrating on, and being sure of the main thrust of the study. Leaders will also probably want to work out approximately how long they'd like to spend on each part.
- We haven't included an 'answer guide' to the questions in the studies. This is a deliberate move. We want to give you a guided tour of Mark's Gospel, not a lecture. There is more than enough in the text we have written and the questions we have asked to point you in what we think is the right direction. The rest is up to you.

For more input:
- See 'Tips for leaders' on page 87.
- There is also a series of audio cassettes available which expound the relevant passages—see page 91ff for more details.

Before you begin

We recommend that before you start study 1 you take the time to read right through Mark in one sitting; it should only take you about 2 hours This will give you a feel for the direction and purpose of the whole book, and help you greatly in placing each passage in its context.

At that time, Jesus

Was Jesus a great prophet and teacher? Was he merely one in a long line of inspired individuals, including Buddha and Mohammed? Did he travel to England as a child? Is he more popular than the Beatles?

These days, it seems possible to find as many different Jesuses as brands of softdrink. Every year there's another book about the 'authentic' Jesus. All the authors have their own theory and they all present it as the most obvious and plausible one. Most have this in common: they disagree with traditional Christianity. How do we deal with this huge range of opinions?

Jesus was an historical figure who lived and died in the first century. He was also a powerful teacher who, in the centuries following his lifetime, has influenced the lives of millions of people from many different nationalities and personal backgrounds. No serious-minded person would disagree with these statements. Yet the full meaning and significance of Jesus remains a contentious issue. Who was he really? And what was he really on about?

For starters

What do people say about Jesus? What opinions do you hear in the media, at work, around about? On what do people base their opinions? Jot down a few answers.

If we want to know the truth about Jesus, there is only one place to turn. We must read and study the Gospels, for they are the only reliable source of detailed information about him.

The Gospel of Mark is probably the earliest of the four Gospels, and was written while many of those who were involved in the events (as participants or eye-witnesses) were still alive. It is a remarkable book, and not only because of its subject matter. The more we read Mark's account of Jesus, the more we are entranced by what a great story it is, and by how well it is told.

It must be said at this point, that many of us are not used to reading Mark's Gospel (or any of the Gospels for that matter) as one continuous *story*. Instead, we are more used to regarding the Gospels as a collection of lots of different stories that don't have much to do with each other. We're familiar with stories about healings and exorcisms, about John the Baptist, about miracles and parables, about arguments with Jewish leaders, and of course about Jesus' death and resurrection. Yet many of us have grown up with these Gospel stories without pausing to think that there might be a connection between all these different incidents, that the Gospel author might be trying to tell a big story of which all the different episodes are only part.

We can be like people who only know a movie by the trailers they see on TV. We have a rough idea what it is about, and have seen the highlights, but we haven't yet grasped how the whole thing holds together, and what the overall point is. In fact, we aren't even sure which movie the episodes come from, since there are four versions of Christ's life, each written from a slightly different perspective, and each containing particular emphases.

These studies are like a trip to see one of these 'movies': the Gospel of Mark. We're not going to simply look at a grab bag of highlights. We're going to see how the whole story fits together, how the characters relate to each other, how one episode flows into the next, and how Mark presents us with a unique portrait of Jesus.

As we do so, we'll see that the Jesus of Mark's Gospel is not only surprising and intriguing—he also fulfils all our grandest dreams.

Let us begin where all stories begin: at the beginning.

The beginning of the Gospel

According to its opening words, Mark's book will tell its readers about "the beginning of the gospel of Jesus Christ, the Son of God". Mark is written for those living after the time of Jesus, to tell them how the Christian message originated. Where did it come from, this 'good news' about a crucified Messiah? What were the events that started it all? Who was this Jesus? What was he on about? And what was he supposed to have done?

Mark immediately identifies Jesus as 'the Christ' and 'the Son of God'. We are so used to these words that we barely pause to consider what they mean. However, for Mark's original readers, these were words full of significance.

'Christ', for example, is not Jesus' surname. It is a title for the long-awaited King of Israel ('Messiah' is the same word in Hebrew.) In the Old Testament God had promised that this king would one day come to defeat all Israel's enemies, and to bring in a new age of prosperity and peace.

The 'Son of God' basically means the same thing. It was another of the titles given to the Kings of Israel, and so is another way of referring to the Christ or Messiah. It is a somewhat confusing title for Christians because we are used to calling Jesus 'God the Son'— that is, the second person of the trinity. But these are two slightly different things. God the Son has always been at the Father's side, from all eternity. When Jesus was born as a man, and lived and died and rose from the dead, he *became* the 'Son of God'—that is, he became the long-awaited Messiah or Christ of Israel.

From the outset, then, Mark tells his readers something that the characters in the story (like the disciples) will take some time to discover. We know from the start that Jesus—the central character—is the Christ (or Messiah), the Son of God. From the start, we know that this is no ordinary story, but concerns the king of all the earth!

What happens next

The royal coach, pulled by four immaculate horses, draws up to the entrance of the great hall. The red carpet is out. Dignitaries wait nervously in the hope of recognition, or even a handshake. The crowd strains forward to catch a glimpse. The footman opens the door and out steps…

We all know what happens next. We all know who to expect. The signs and trappings of royalty are unmistakable.

Yet when Jesus began his public ministry, what did people expect? What were the signs? Was the red carpet out?

Jesus the Messiah certainly did not arrive in a vacuum, unexpected and unannounced. On the contrary, he had been expected for hundreds of years. And if we are to understand anything about Jesus, we must understand something of the expectations that surrounded his arrival, and the kingdom he would bring.

In fact, Mark begins his story by telling us from the Old Testament just who was expected, and what was meant to happen once he arrived.

What happens next...
...according to the Old Testament?

Investigate

Read Malachi 3:1-5. (Mark 1:2 is a quote from Malachi 3:1)
1. What does Malachi prophesy will happen first?

2. What is supposed to happen after that?

Read Isaiah 40:1-11. (Mark 1:3 is a quote from Isaiah 40:3)
3. What does Isaiah prophesy will happen first?

4. What is supposed to happen after that?

5. How would you summarize the promise of these Old Testament verses?

What happens next...
...according to John

As soon as Mark finishes quoting these prophecies, he introduces John the Baptist (Mark 1:4-8).

Investigate

Read Mark 1:4-8.

1. Why did the people come to John? What were they looking for?

2. John is portrayed by Mark as the 'messenger' of the Old Testament prophecies. According to John's message, what will happen next?

3. According to the Old Testament prophecies we looked at above, who was supposed to come after him?

'Baptism in the Spirit'

Two common mistakes can be made here. The 'baptism in the Holy Spirit' is neither referring to Christian baptismal practices, nor to what pentecostals refer to as 'the second blessing'. Both mistakes try to read later church phenomena back into the Gospel. Instead, we must understand John's reference to baptism in the light of the situation in Jesus' time. Notice that John compares a symbol (what he does) with the reality (what the stronger one will do). 'Baptism' simply means a washing, which is a natural symbol for cleansing or purification. 'Baptism in the Holy Spirit' is the cleansing or purifying that God will do. This is what people wanted (1:4-5), and what the Old Testament had promised. Later on, Jesus will reveal that the 'baptism' he performs according to God's plan is his death (10:38, 45).

What happens next...
...according to God

The words are barely out of John's mouth, when Mark introduces the very One John had been speaking about:

> At that time Jesus came from Nazareth in Galilee and was baptised by John in the Jordan. (Mark 1:9)

In a dramatic scene, Jesus is endowed with the Holy Spirit and hears a voice from heaven, saying, "You are my Son, whom I love; with you I am well pleased".

This short sentence seems a straightforward thing to say. God is declaring from heaven that he loves his Son, and that he is very pleased with him. But there is more to it than that. God is repeating words that he had spoken many hundreds of years earlier in the Old Testament. God is quoting from two Old Testament passages, one about his Son whom he loves, and another about a 'servant' who would receive the Spirit and be well-pleasing to God.

Investigate

Read Psalm 2.

1. What should happen once God's Son, the king of Israel, is established on his throne?

Read Isaiah 42:1-4.

2. When the Spirit-filled servant arrives, what will happen next?

3. There are three other passages about this servant in Isaiah. Quickly read them. What do they tell us about the ministry of the Servant?

Isaiah 49:1-7

Isaiah 50:4-11

Isaiah 52:13-53:12

What happens next...
...according to Jesus

In this climate of expectation, with all these promises and prophecies in the air, and with John the Baptist pointing to him as the One they'd been waiting for, Jesus begins to proclaim his message: "The time has come. The kingdom of God is near. Repent and believe the good news!" (Mark 1:14-15).

According to Jesus, the time has finally come. The prophecies are about to be fulfilled. The long-awaited kingdom is near. And since this is all about to happen, it is a time for urgent and immediate action.

According to Jesus, two things will happen next: 1) the kingdom will come; and 2) his hearers will have to make their minds up how to respond—either accepting his message (by repenting and believing) or rejecting it.

Think it through

1. If someone asked you, "Who is Jesus?", how would you reply? How has this study affected your answer?

2. Imagine that you have never read Mark's Gospel, nor even heard the story of Jesus. What do you expect to happen next as Mark's Gospel unfolds?

3. Why should every person alive take a good look at Jesus?

2

As one who had authority

So far in Mark's Gospel, we have been awaiting the arrival of the king. Mark has told us from the outset that his book is all about Jesus, the king, the Messiah. We have been reminded of the Old Testament expectations, and heard the testimony of John the Baptist and even God himself at Jesus' baptism.

Now the king has stepped from the carriage onto the waiting red carpet and announced his arrival ('the kingdom of God is near'). One thing remains: What will the king do? How will he act? How will he wield his royal power?

In this next section of Mark's Gospel, we not only begin to see the royal authority of Jesus the Messiah in action, we also see him start to interact with his subjects. Mark introduces us to the different characters who will figure in the dramatic story to follow.

Four encounters with authority

Investigate

(If you are studying in a group you may like to break into four groups and take one of the following passages each, then report back.)

1. The Fishermen

Read Mark 1:16-20.
a. What does Jesus promise to do for these men?

b. If they follow him, what are the consequences?

c. What does this encounter tell us about Jesus the king?

2. The Synagogue

Read Mark 1:21-28.
a. Why are people impressed by Jesus in Capernaum?

b. What does the evil spirit know that the crowd does not know?

c. What does this encounter tell us about Jesus the king?

3. The sick

Read Mark 1:29-39.
a. How is Jesus' authority shown in this section?

b. From Jesus' actions and words, what did he think his mission was all about?

4. The leper

Read Mark 1:40-45.
a. Why do you think the leper was hesitant about asking for healing?

b. What do you find surprising about this incident?

c. What does Jesus' encounter with the leper tell us about the sort of king he is?

These passages certainly show what a remarkable person Jesus was. The fishermen left their ordinary life, their work, their family, and at this stage they did not even know where Jesus was heading! There must have been something compelling about Jesus to command such a response. Obviously his healings drew people's attention—but notice that although Jesus was able to heal, and had sympathy for the ill, it was not his primary interest. He left the huge crowd to go further afield with his preaching about the coming kingdom (vv. 38-39).

In many respects, we modern readers are distracted by the fact that Jesus could heal at all. We are so struck by his power, that we can easily overlook how astounding it was for him to *touch* someone with leprosy, someone defiled and 'unclean' under the religious law of the time. The leper certainly did not expect it; he doubted Jesus' willingness to heal (not his ability).

Jesus has already been contrasted with the religious leaders of the day (v. 22). In the next series of stories, this contrast becomes open conflict.

Authority opposed

Investigate

Read Mark 2:1-12.
1. What is the source of Jesus' authority?

2. What is Jesus' authority for?

3. What were the responses to Jesus' words (and the actions that backed them up)?

The 'Son of Man' is the way Jesus refers to himself. It could be that this is just a roundabout way of speaking, much as one can use 'one' in referring to oneself. It is hardly a coincidence, however, that the 'Son of Man' was also the name given to a man in Daniel 7 who came to God (v. 13) and was given the kingdom of God (v. 14; cf. Daniel 2:44). He therefore had authority over all people.

4. Read the following passages in Mark and fill in the table

	What opposition does Jesus face?	(If relevant) How does Jesus answer the opposition?
2:13-17		
2:18-20		
2:23-28		
3:1-6		
3:20-21		
3:31-34		

To sum up: what is the difference between Jesus' attitude and that of his opponents?

Read Mark 3:22-29.
In this scene, the religious leaders oppose Jesus to his face. They question the source of his authority (vv. 22, 30).

5. How does Jesus' riddle answer their charge (vv. 23-27)?

6. Why does Jesus give them such a stern warning (vv. 28-30)?

Blaspheming against the Holy Spirit
This passage has often worried Christians. "What if I blaspheme the Holy Spirit?"

We need to look carefully at what is actually being said. Jesus was accused of being from Satan. This is utter blasphemy, for Jesus' authority does not come from Satan, but from God. Jesus is the one upon whom the Spirit came, the Son, the Servant of the Lord (1:9-11). If people reject him, they "blaspheme the Spirit". Jesus is the Son of Man, with the authority to forgive sins on earth (2:10). If the religious leaders reject him, they reject the only source of forgiveness and will therefore remain guilty of eternal sin.

Reacting to authority
The people of Jesus' day were confronted with a choice. They had traditionally found out about God by following their authorised religious leaders. But now a new teacher had arrived on the scene, one who oozed authority in everything he said and did. How would they react? Would their amazement lead them to "repent and believe the good news", as Jesus had challenged them to do?

These are the questions waiting to be answered as we read on.

Think it through

1. From what we have read so far in Mark, what was Jesus offering people if they followed him?

2. What does Jesus offer us today that religious leaders cannot equal?

3. What is radical about Jesus' authority?

3

This is what the kingdom will be like

For starters

1. Through the media and your daily contact with people, what do you think is the most pressing issue for people in our society today?

2. What are people trying to gain for the future by battling with this issue?

3. What chances do you think they have of success? Is there any assurance that their hopes will be realised?

4. What is your own most pressing hope for the future? What do you long for and dream about most?

Most human dreams remain just that—dreams. In fact, the harder we work towards them, and the more we strive, the more elusive they can be.

Jesus also had a dream for the future, except it was not so much a dream as a plan. He knew it would happen, and the challenge he put before people was to believe that it was going to happen, and to change their lives accordingly.

What was it that Jesus was expecting? What sort of future was he banking on? And how did he expect it to come about?

Chapter 4 of Mark's Gospel has Jesus beginning to explain what the future kingdom of God will be like, and why only some will enter it.

The prophecies of the kingdom

Once again, to understand this next section of Mark, we need to acquaint ourselves with the Old Testament background that lies behind it. The prophets of the Old Testament had great hopes for the future kingdom God would establish. Let us delve into some of them.

Investigate

1. Read the following passages. What does each passage expect will happen?

Daniel 2:44

Daniel 7:13-14

Daniel 7:17-18, 26-27

Daniel 12:1-4

2. How does this kingdom meet the longings of humanity?

3. Read the following verses. When was the kingdom of God expected?

Daniel 12:1-4; 8-9; 13

Mark 1:14-15

There are many Old Testament passages which describe the kingdom to come, and we have looked at only a sample. The people of Israel knew that God did not intend this world to be all there is. There was promised a future time when all the troubles of life—in particular, political enemies and the sinful behaviour of the people—would be done away with. Then God's people would rule forever in a glorious kingdom in which God himself would have an undefiled and open relationship with his people.

It was all something far-off, distant, at the end of time. Most of the Old Testament prophecies were vague about the timing; it would happen "on that day" (the day of judgement) or "at the end". It was certain; but it was not yet.

As a prophet, it would not have been at all unusual for Jesus to preach about God's kingdom. His preaching, however, had a dramatic twist—he said the kingdom was near! The long wait was over. The time was suddenly accelerating, and the climax was approaching. If the kingdom was so near, what would it be like? And how was it going to arrive?

The parables of the kingdom

Investigate

Read Mark 4:1-34.
1. Look back over verses 1-20. Jesus has been preaching the "good news of God" (1:14-15). What does the parable of the sower say about potential responses to the announcement of this news?

2. Look back over verses 21-22.

   a. What does this parable lead you to expect?

   b. What does it say about Jesus' ministry?

3. The lesson of this parable is reinforced by the saying in verses 24-25. What is the promise and the warning of these verses?

4. Look back over verses 26-29.

    a. What does this parable lead you to expect?

    b. What does this say about the kingdom?

5. Look back over verses 30-32. What does this parable lead you to expect?

The world tree

The 'tree' image is used in other places in the Bible to stand for a kingdom. In Daniel 4:9-12 and 19-22, a tree is a symbol of a kingdom that exercises world dominion (also see Ezek 17:22-24). It is a tree that spreads its branches over all. In Mark 4, the largeness of the plant that grows from the mustard seed points to the worldwide spread of the kingdom. As the Old Testament expected, the kingdom of God would involve all kinds of people and not just in Israel—all the nations of the world would be included.

6. In summary, what would these parables lead you to expect?

The kingdom of God as taught by Jesus has some surprising characteristics. It is not going to come by political conquest or force; it has elements of secrecy and slow hidden growth. At the same time, something about it is to be openly disclosed (vv. 22-23).

There is also a hint that some will be inside it, and some outside. There will be those like the bad soils, who either never listen at all (v. 15) or do not take it seriously (vv. 16-19); or those whose ears are closed, who will hear but never understand (v. 12). It is as if Jesus is saying that the kingdom is there for those who want it; but there will be those who will turn away.

The kingdom is certainly coming, says Jesus. It is inevitable, as surely as reaping follows sowing. We therefore need to get ready for it–urgently–if we are to be part of God's future.

Think it through

1. What does the gospel of Jesus say to our world which is filled with hopes and dreams for a better future?

2. Why will some not listen? What is it about the kingdom that they will not like?

3. What might keep you from the kingdom? How can you prevent it?

The sheep and their shepherds

One of the remarkable benefits of democracy is that it allows us to remove our political leaders regularly. We don't have to resort to civil war or royal beheadings. All it takes is a nice, orderly election which is arranged for us by the political leaders themselves every few years.

It is curious that we feel the need for this constant changeover of leadership. Surely, on a purely practical level, it would make more sense for the leadership to be long term, to have time to consolidate, to plan for the future and effect some real change. It seems, however, that we have an innate distrust of our leaders. Perhaps this is because they so regularly let us down. They do not keep their promises; they appear to act selfishly and not in the best interest of the country; indeed, we have political leaders these days who openly state that they lie as a matter of course.

It is not only a modern problem. Human leaders, whether political, religious or social, have a sad history of corruption, failure, neglect and self-interest. It was the same in the Israel of Jesus' time; but there it was even more serious, for Israel's leaders had a special mandate from God to look after his chosen people. Their failure, in contrast with Jesus, is the focus of this study.

Before we begin, a word of explanation about the next few studies. In this study and the next two, we will look at the large middle section of Mark that runs from chapter 4 verse 35 right through to the end of chapter 10. It's a little hard to divide these chapters up neatly into chunks for study, because the episodes are all so interconnected, and gain much of their meaning from their relation to one another. In order to get some feel for this, the passages we will read in this study and the next two will overlap with one another somewhat.

Jesus the powerful shepherd

Investigate

Read Mark 4:35-41.
1. What does the episode show us about Jesus' strength and authority?

2. Why do the disciples ask their question (v. 41)?

3. Of what were they afraid?

Read Psalm 107:23-32.
4. How does this add meaning to Jesus' actions in the boat?

Read Mark 5:1-20.
5. In the description of the man, what is emphasised?

6. Look back at Mark 3:23-27 where Jesus answers the accusation that he himself is possessed by Satan. In light of this, what have we learnt about Jesus from his encounter with the demoniac?

7. Compare words used to describe Jesus in Mark 5, verses 19 and 20. Who did Mark think Jesus was?

Jesus crosses back over the sea and is again confronted by a group of people who are suffering from the physical effects of the fallen world. Again we see Jesus' strength. *Read Mark 5:21-43.*

8. Jairus is a synagogue ruler, one of the religious leaders of his people, yet he is powerless to save his daughter. What does he expect from Jesus? What does he get?

9. The woman with bleeding was also powerless, and beyond the help of anyone else. What response does Jesus commend her for?

Read Mark 6:1-6.
10. What is so strange about the response in Nazareth?

11. What are the reasons for the people's response?

Israel's failed shepherds

Immediately following these demonstrations of Jesus' strength, we have passages telling us about Israel's official leadership—first Herod (in 6:14-29) and then the Pharisees (in 7:1-16). And sandwiched in between these two passages about Israel's leaders, we again see the power and compassion of Jesus, the true and faithful Shepherd of Israel (in 6:30-57). Mark often uses this sort of device in his Gospel (and we will see more of it in the coming chapters). He links together different incidents in order to make a point. He sets up contrasts and comparisons, sometimes between Jesus and the religious authorities, and sometimes between the disciples and other people who are responding to Jesus.

Lying very prominently in the background to this whole section is the prophecy of Ezekiel.

Investigate

Read Ezekiel 34:1-6.
1. What should the shepherds of Israel have been doing?

2. What were they doing instead?

3. What had happened to the sheep?

4. Does anything in this passage sound like what Jesus has been doing?

Read Ezekiel 34:11-16, 20-24.
5. What did God promise to do for his flock?

6. Whom would he send?

Read Mark 6:14-29.
7. Is Herod an attractive or an unattractive character? What are his strengths and weaknesses?

8. What threat does Herod pose for Jesus' mission?

Read Mark 6:30-44.
9. What phrase in this passage reminds us of Ezekiel 34?

10. Also look up Numbers 27:15-18. Given that 'Joshua' is simply the Hebrew form of 'Jesus', what is being said about Jesus in Mark 6?

11. How is Jesus being contrasted with Herod? What does Jesus do that Herod doesn't do?

Read Mark 7:1-8.
12. What problem does Jesus expose in Israel's leaders?

13. Why are the leaders hard-hearted?

14. Overall, what is Jesus' assessment of Israel's leadership?

In Ezekiel 34, God promised to come to his people, to search for the lost, to gather the strays, and to feed them. He also promised to send another 'David', another great shepherd-king who would care for his people.

Who then is Jesus? He is clearly portrayed in these chapters as God's alternative to the corrupt leadership of Israel. He is the one who has compassion on the scattered sheep. But is he the Lord who has come to gather his people? Or is he the 'David', the Messiah, come to be their prince? Or is he perhaps both?

To this we turn in our next study.

Think it through

1. What makes a leader worth following?

2. What makes Jesus a leader worth following?

3. What is the proper response to him?

4. Why do people not give that response?

5 *Who do you say I am?*

In our last study we saw the contrast between Jesus and Israel's leadership. With the arrival of Jesus, God is coming to replace the corrupt and failed leadership of Israel with his own good shepherd in the line of David.

All the while, we the readers know who Jesus really is. Mark has told us from the very first sentence of the book that Jesus is God's Messiah, the king, come to bring God's long-awaited kingdom.

However, for the characters in the story—like the disciples, the crowds, the people Jesus meets, his family, the religious authorities—it's not so simple. They are still trying to work out exactly what is going on, and just who this amazing man is. Some of them will get it right. Others won't.

This is another constant theme throughout these chapters—will the characters work out who Jesus really is? In particular, will the disciples, with whom we identify most, put their trust in Jesus? Or will they be hard-hearted and go the way of the Pharisees? And what about us? How will we respond?

The heart problem

In chapter 6, Jesus crosses the sea for a second time with his disciples (as he did in chapter 4:35-41, and as he will again in chapter 8:13-21). Once again, he astounds them by revealing himself to them in a unique way.

Investigate

1. Modern readers without a solid Old Testament background may miss some of the points that Mark makes as he describes this event. Read Mark 6:45-56, and then look up the following Old Testament references that add meaning to the incident. Remember that this is not a matter of proof-texting, but recognizing that Mark is deliberately using language (describing what Jesus actually did) which should spark off Old Testament images in your mind. As the picture builds up, draw your own conclusions: Who is this man?

He walked on the sea: Psalm 77:19

He was about to pass them by: Exodus 33:19, 22; 34:6

He provoked fear: Exodus 20:18-21

He told them not to fear: Isaiah 41:13; 43:1-3; 44:2

He said "It is I" or, better translated, "I AM": Exodus 3:14, Isaiah 41:4

He seemed to calm the wind: Psalm 65:7; 107:25-30

2. Why do the disciples respond as they do? What is their problem?

3. Go back and quickly re-read the first sea-crossing incident in Mark 4:35-41. Have the disciples progressed at all in their understanding?

Now read Mark 7:1-30.
4. What is the real problem of the religious leaders?

5. How do Jesus' disciples compare with the religious leaders (remember 4:40; 6:52)?

6. The Syrophonecian woman is a Greek. As Jesus points out to her, she is a foreigner to Israel. She is one of the 'dogs', one of the unclean, with whom Jews were not to associate. Given all this, how does the woman's response to Jesus compare with those we have just seen? What is the state of her heart?

Hearing and sight problems

Investigate

Read Mark 7:31-8:26.

1. What is your impression of the disciples during the feeding of the four thousand (given the previous feeding in chapter 6)?

2. When Jesus again crosses the sea with them (in 8:13-21), what does he warn them about?

3. How do you think this danger might explain the difference between the two feedings (compare Mark 6:4-6)?

4. What problems do the disciples have, according to Jesus?

5. What is unusual about the healing of the blind man (in 8:22-26)? How is this a picture of the disciples?

6. Look again at the stories which surround this conversation in the boat. If the disciples are ever to understand, what must happen to them?

The solution

In the marvellous way that Mark weaves together the different strands of his account, a stunning picture emerges—not only of the compassionate majesty and power of Jesus, but also of the quite incredible hostility of the religious authorities, and the baffling stupidity of his closest associates.

The disciples just do not understand. God himself has come amongst them, the promises of Scripture are being fulfilled, yet Jesus' own followers—like Israel's leaders—are too dull to see it. Both the deaf mute and the blind man are pictures of the disciples. They have ears but do not hear. They have eyes but do not see. They need someone to heal them, to open the deaf ears and blind eyes.

Fortunately for the disciples, there is someone among them who can do just that. And in the following passage, in chapter 8:27-30, this is what happens. Like the mute whom Jesus healed, Peter's tongue is loosened and he begins to speak plainly. He confesses what we (as readers) have known all along: "You are the Christ". At last, the disciples openly recognize who Jesus is.

This is the climax of the Gospel thus far. As we shall see, it is also the turning point, for from this point on the story takes an amazing twist.

Think it through

1. We tend to think of the Pharisees as the 'bad guys' in the story. But what would have been their standing in the community of their day? How do you think they would have been regarded?

2. The disciples were for a time just like the Pharisees and Herod. Have you seen people reacting to Jesus like this?

3. What is necessary before people can understand who Jesus is?

4. How does this make you think about:

• your own knowledge of Jesus?

• how you can help other people who don't know Jesus?

6

What must I do?

For starters

1. Think about the most impressive Christian people you know. What makes them stand out?

2. If you were to ask most people today, what would they say is the essence of 'being a Christian'?

So far in Mark's story, we have witnessed the arrival of the king—that is, Jesus, God's Messiah. Even the slow-witted disciples have begun to realise this.

But what sort of kingdom is Jesus about to establish? How will he do it? And what does he want from his followers?

As we shall see in this study, these questions are all related. And as Jesus begins to answer them, the disciples are in for a surprise.

Investigate

Read Mark 8:27-9:1.
1. What does Peter now see (v. 29)?

2. What does he not yet see (vv. 31-33)?

3. What lies in front of Jesus?

4. What does he want from his followers?

5. Why would his followers possibly be ashamed of Jesus?

6. Why does Jesus make such an urgent demand?

Read Mark 9:2-13.
7. On the mountain the three disciples are given a glimpse of Jesus' glory. What are they reminded about? (v. 7, cf 1:11)

8. What will happen to Jesus?

The extraordinary events on the mountain only reinforce the message that the disciples have found so unacceptable—namely, that despite all his glory and power, and despite the fact that he is God's Messiah, Jesus faces suffering, rejection and death at the hands of Israel's leaders. It must happen, for Scripture says so.

Jesus points out to them that the Elijah figure (John the Baptist) has already come first, as the Scriptures said he would—and has suffered at the hands of the very people meant to be expecting him. Accordingly, the only thing left to happen before the kingdom of God arrives is that the Son of Man must also suffer. He will then rise from the dead, at which time the disciples can tell others what they had seen (9:9).

True to their form thus far, the three disciples do not understand Jesus' teaching. They have not grasped why the Christ has to suffer. Peter would rather keep the glory while it's there (9:5)—he has not understood that glory must come by way of the cross.

In the episodes that follow, this theme continues to be played out. Just what is the right response to Jesus? What does he want from his followers?

Investigate

Read Mark 9:14-10:31 and fill in the table overleaf as you go.

Incident	What attitude or response does Jesus commend?	What attitude or response does Jesus condemn?
Healing the boy (9:14-32)		
Who is the greatest? (9:33-37)		
Not against us is for us (9:38-41)		
Kingdom or hell (9:42-50)		
Pharisees & divorce (10:1-12)		
The children (10:13-16)		
The rich man (10:17-31)		
Suffering & servanthood (10:32-45)		
Blind Bartimaeus (10:46-52)		

Think it through

Think back over this whole section (from 8:27-10:52).

1. What is Jesus' repeated message to the disciples about what must happen to him before the kingdom comes?

2. What sort of Messiah is Jesus? How will he bring in his kingdom?

3. How is this related to entering the kingdom? What is the only way into the kingdom?

4. Who are the best examples of this response in this section?

5. Who are the worst examples?

Like the previous section of Mark's Gospel, this section also finishes with a blind man being healed—but there is an important difference between the two. The first (in 8:22-26) is healed in two stages. At first, he sees, and yet does not quite see. This is a picture of the disciples. They finally realise that Jesus is the Messiah/Christ, yet they are still rather blurry about how he will bring in the kingdom and what they must do to enter it. They believe, and yet they need to overcome their unbelief (like the father of the boy with the evil spirit).

The second blind man (Bartimaeus in 10:46-52) is a model of true discipleship. He hears about Jesus, immediately asks for mercy (and only mercy), and having received it, follows Jesus along the road to Jerusalem where Jesus will be crucified.

The children are the same. They are not great or rich or powerful or prestigious. They simply come to Jesus to receive a blessing, and he receives them gladly. Their dependency and trust are what makes them such classic examples of what it means to enter the kingdom.

Woven throughout these examples of right and wrong responses to Jesus is the constant prediction by Jesus of his suffering and death. This culminates in 10:45 where Jesus explains that he has come as the 'servant' (as in Isaiah 53) who will give his life as a ransom for many. When he dies, it will be as a sacrifice for sins, to take away the debt that is owing, to pay the price of freedom for the many. This is the necessary cost of bringing in his kingdom, for if sinners are going to enter it, they must receive mercy; and if God is going to dispense mercy, then sin must be paid for.

In other words, this whole section links together two crucial ideas:

- that in defiance of people's expectations, the Messiah will bring in the kingdom by suffering, dying and rising again, as a ransom to pay for the sins of many;
- that in defiance of people's expectations, the way to enter the kingdom of Jesus is through humble dependence and faith; the way to be great in the kingdom is to be a lowly servant.

Not that this will be easy. Following Jesus means being willing to forgo anything that keeps us from the kingdom. We must be prepared to give up everything, lose everything, and only depend on Jesus. Our Christ was the one who died to become King. Being in the kingdom means going the way of the cross. It will be hard—but it will be worth it.

Think it through

1. When we talk about 'following Jesus', we normally mean something like 'obeying Jesus' teaching' or 'living a good life after his example'. What does 'following Jesus' mean in this part of Mark? Where were people following him to?

2. What does this mean for our own life? How would you summarise the essence of the Christian life having read this part of Mark's Gospel?

3. Throughout this section of Mark, what are the things that get in the way of people responding rightly to Jesus? Which of these is most relevant to you?

4. According to Jesus, true greatness in his kingdom lies in servanthood, just as he came not to be served but to serve. Think about how this might be worked out:

- in your own life and relationships with people

- in your church

7

Mark 11-12

He overturned the tables

For starters

1. Every time someone has an opinion about Jesus, it means they are judging him. For instance, some people say they will only believe Jesus is Lord if you can prove it is reasonable and rational to do so. Think for a moment about how people judge Jesus. What standards or yardsticks do people use to assess Him? Jot down a few answers.

Chapters 11 and 12 of Mark's Gospel cover three days of action in Jerusalem. As Jesus interacts with people, we begin to see that judging Jesus can be a dangerous business. He has a habit of turning the tables, and putting his accusers in the dock.

Day one: the coming king

Investigate

Read Mark 11:1-11.
1. What does Jesus do on day one?

2. What are people expecting when he arrives in Jerusalem? (cf Zechariah 9:9)

Day two: the ruined kingdom?

Investigate

Read Mark 11:12-19.
1. What does Jesus do on day two?

2. What impression of Israel do these events convey?

3. Look up the two Old Testament passages quoted in verse 17 to see what light they shed on the events.

    a. Isaiah 56:4-8. What should the temple have been for?

    b Jeremiah 7:1-11. Who was Jeremiah prophesying against? And what were they doing wrong?

4. Who is Jesus criticising?

At first glance, the cursing of the fig-tree seems quite bizarre. Why would Jesus do such a thing?

Like so many of the incidents recorded for us in Mark's Gospel, the cursing of the fig-tree takes its meaning partly from its Old Testament background, and partly from its place in the story that Mark is telling.

In the Old Testament (in Micah 7), the fruitless fig-tree is likened to Israel, in which there is not one godly person. Sure enough, in Mark 11, immediately after Jesus curses the barren fig-tree, he enters Jerusalem only to find it equally unprepared for his arrival. Jerusalem too is barren. Instead of the temple being a house of prayer, it is a den of robbers. Corruption is rampant. Instead of the temple being a beacon for the nations, and for all the outcast, to come and meet the Lord, it has become a place of empty ritual and commercial greed. The Lord arrives at his temple, and finds his people blind to his identity and presence. They are more interested in making a buck!

The Old Testament prophets laid the blame for Israel's decline on the leaders of Israel, and it appears that Jesus agrees. The high priests and their entourage are especially singled out for his wrath. The leadership of Israel has let Israel down. Like the fig-tree, it was 'not the season for fruit', because Israel's leadership has caused the ruin of Israel.

Day three: Who is the judge?

Investigate

Read Mark 11:27-12:44.
1. Jot down a quick summary of what happens on day three.

2. Fill in this table:

	How do they attack Jesus?	On what basis does Jesus reply?	What is the outcome?
Teachers of the law & elders			
Pharisees & Herodians			
Sadducees			

3. Overall, who is the victor thus far? Do you expect that this is the end of the conflict?

4. What was different about the teacher's question in verse 28?

The tension between Jesus and the religious leaders that has been simmering throughout Mark's Gospel is exploding into full-scale conflict. For his part, Jesus warns people that the religious leaders are dangerous hypocrites. They are even "devouring widows' houses", the very people the leadership of Israel were supposed to specially protect. The little incident at the temple treasury is a case in point (12:41-44). Here is a widow whose house is devoured. While the rich are relatively unharmed, she has to put everything that she has into paying the religious authorities' temple tax. Israel's leadership is ruining Israel!

Jesus defeats Israel's leaders and obviously knows more about the Christ than they do. He appears to be firmly in charge throughout the whole day's activities. And yet we have still ringing in our ears Jesus' predictions (in chapters 8-10) that these religious leaders will eventually persecute and kill him. The irony is that in thus judging Jesus, they will be judged themselves:

> "What then will the owner of the vineyard do? He will come and kill those tenants and give the vineyard to others. Haven't you read this scripture: 'The stone the builders rejected has become the capstone; the Lord has done this, and it is marvellous in our eyes'?" (Mark 12:9-11).

Think it through

1. How do the events of chapters 11-12 illustrate Mark 4:24-25?

2. Why do people reject Jesus today?

3. The really important question these chapters pose is: What is *our* judgement of Jesus? How would you answer the question in Mark 11:28?

When will these things happen?

Show me a sign

Perhaps it stems from our longing for certainty about the future, or it might be simply a result of our unfailing human curiosity, but passages like Mark 13 have always held a particular fascination for Christians—along with parts of Daniel, Zechariah, Ezekiel, 2 Thessalonians and almost the whole of Revelation. Whenever the Bible addresses the future of human history, and speaks somewhat cryptically of when and how it will unfold, we cannot help ourselves. We instinctively want to unlock the mystery, decipher the symbols, and work out exactly what will happen and when. Indeed, Christian history is littered with the strange doctrines, millennial speculations, schisms and controversies which have arisen from the intensity of this desire to have the future revealed.

The disciples of Jesus certainly have the future in mind when they leave Jerusalem at the beginning Mark 13. Things don't look so good between Jesus and the religious authorities. Trouble is brewing. The predictions of Jesus about his suffering and death, so strange and unthinkable in chapter 8, now seem more likely, if not inevitable.

One of the disciples tries to comfort Jesus by referring to the majesty of the temple. However, as Jesus responds, and the conversation continues, it becomes apparent that, once again, the disciples don't really know what's going on.

Investigate

Read Mark 13:1-4.

1. Why would the disciple have considered his remark (in v.1) to be an encouraging thing to say to Jesus? (Ps 48:12-14 will help you answer this.)

2. How do you think Jesus' reply (in v. 2) would have been received by the disciples? How is this reflected in their double-barrelled question of verse 4?

3. Compare Mark 8:11-13. Is this the sort of question the disciples should have been asking? Is there anything wrong with their attitude?

Read Mark 13:5-13.

4. What danger does Jesus warn them about?

5. What specific difficulties will the disciples face?

6. Why would these difficulties make Jesus' warning all the more important?

7. What will keep the disciples going?

Read Mark 13:14-23.
8. What are the disciples told to do when they see the awful horror of verse 14? Why the urgency?

9. In this time of great distress, there will be people who offer a dangerous threat to the disciples. Why are they such a threat? (21-22, cf 8:27-30)

10. In view of the troubled times that lay ahead for them, why is the disciples' original question (in v. 4) a dangerous one? (cf vv. 21-23)

If the disciples thought that the destruction of the temple was an alarming prospect, Jesus tells them, "You ain't seen nothin' yet!". The catastrophe that is coming will involve the greatest time of distress this world has ever seen or will ever see (v. 19). It will be so severe that the Lord will have to limit it, for the sake of the elect (v. 20). Daniel had been told about this great distress before the end-time resurrection (Daniel 12:1-4). He had been told that this would happen a long way in the future (Daniel 12:9), but now the disciples are told that they would experience these things in their own life-time!

The book of Daniel is much in the background of this passage. The "abomination that causes desolation" of verse 14 is an allusion to Daniel 9:27, 11:31 and 12:11. When Jesus says, "let the reader understand", he probably means, "understand that what Daniel spoke of, I am now warning you about". The emphasis is upon the "abomination" or "horror" or "sacrilege". Jesus is warning the disciples that something absolutely horrendous is coming...and soon.

Jesus returns to his warning (v. 23) which shows that this has been his concern for the entire passage so far. The disciples asked a 'sign-seeking question' (in v. 4), and this is why Jesus warns them so sternly. In the difficult times to follow, there would be people who would deny their previous identification of Jesus as the Christ, and who may even offer signs to back up their claims (cf. Deut 13:1-5). If the disciples were sign-seekers, then this would be a powerful temptation for them to desert Jesus as their Christ, especially given that this temptation would come at a time of severe personal distress.

Jesus resets the disciples' sights. Rather than looking out for signs (v. 4), or for 'proof' of what is going to happen, they are to have certain general expectations. They are to be on the alert for the catastrophic things that are about to take place.

Investigate

1. List the things the disciples will see, and any references to timing:

verses 14-23:

verses 24-25:

verse 26:

verse 27:

verses 28-29:

verse 30:

verse 32:

2. **Read Mark 13:32-37.** Since the exact timing is unknown, what should the disciples do?

When will 'these things' happen?

Although the disciples were wrong to ask for 'signs' or proofs of what was to happen in the future, it wasn't wrong for them to ask 'when'. Jesus seems happy to answer that question, and he does so by saying: "No-one knows exactly when, but it's not far away–and certainly within your life-time".

This has led Christians to puzzle over exactly what Jesus meant. Was he talking about the end of the world? Those who think that he was, take verse 26 to refer to the second coming of Christ ("At that time men will see the Son of Man coming in clouds with great power and glory"). Verses 5-23 then become a description of the great distress which is to precede this event, including the coming of the Antichrist who is symbolically referred to as "the abomination of desolation" (v. 14). The difficulty with this view, of course, is that Jesus solemnly declares in verse 30 that these events would happen within the lifetime of that generation. And they plainly didn't.

The other main approach to the passage says that verse 26 should be read in the same way as in Daniel 7:13-14—that is, that the Son of Man comes *to* God, not to earth. This would then apply to the resurrection, ascension and exaltation of Jesus. However, this view then goes on to say that Jesus' exaltation is demonstrated through the destruction of Jerusalem in AD 70. Verses 5-23 are taken to describe the lead up to the destruction of Jerusalem, and it is only at verse 32 that Jesus begins to speak about his second coming. This approach has two problems. Firstly, it gives enormous and somewhat dubious theological weight to the destruction of Jerusalem, an historical event beyond the time of Jesus; and secondly, it has Jesus changing the subject (from the destruction of the temple to his second coming) without any real indication in the text that he is doing so.

These two approaches to the difficulties of Mark 13 have this in common: they look for the solution *outside* Mark's Gospel (either in the return of Christ or in the destruction of Jerusalem). But given how cleverly and purposefully Mark has told his story up till now, why would he break the spell at this crucial point? Why would he start addressing other events quite beyond the lifetime of Jesus? Is it possible that the predictions and warnings of Mark 13 actually refer to what is about to happen next in the story?

A careful reading of the text (and the rest of the story that follows) shows that this is very possible. It is right to take verse 26 as referring to the resurrection and exaltation of Jesus (which Jesus has already predicted in earlier chapters), but there is no need to interpret verses 5-23 as being about the fall of Jerusalem. According to the passage, this time of horrendous distress and appalling sacrilege will happen before the 'coming of the Son of Man'. What terrible event—the worst event in human history—was to happen before the exaltation of Jesus? Put like this, the answer seems obvious: that Israel's leaders should reject, mock and persecute their Messiah, and hand him over to the Gentiles to be humiliated, flogged and crucified. What could be more desolating and abominable than the death of God's own Son at the hands of God's people?

If this way of reading Mark 13 is right, then verses 32-37 also make good sense. In warning the disciples to be on their guard, Jesus refers to the four watches of the night: evening, midnight, cock-crow and dawn. These specific time references only serve to heighten the disciples alertness. When evening comes, they will ask "Well, is it all about to happen?". And when evening passes, and midnight comes, they will ask the same question—only even more intensely, because evening has already passed and there was no fulfilment.

In fact, these four time references provide the structure for the chapters that follow. Jesus meets with the disciples in the upper room at "evening" (14:17); he agonizes in Gethsemane and is betrayed in the middle of the night (14:32-42); he is deserted by his closest friends at "cock-crow" (14:72); and the women go to his empty tomb at "dawn" (16:2).

Mark 13 raises certain expectations, and they are in fact fulfilled within Mark's Gospel. As we read on, we will see Jesus' predictions coming true, not only about his resurrection and exaltation, but also about the terrible abomination that must come first—Jesus' death.

Lessons for the future

Regardless of how we interpret the details, Mark 13 has some important lessons for us about how we regard the future, and how we deal with the suffering and difficulty that inevitably awaits us.

Firstly, we must be wary of the attitude that looks for a sign. To demand a sign is itself a sign—of unbelief. Like the disciples (and unlike the Pharisees), we must trust in Jesus, and believe what he tells about the future. And we must do so without demanding confirmation through signs.

Secondly, we must expect our future to contain suffering. Whenever Christians try to stand firm for the gospel, there will be hardship. There will always be false Christs trying to lead us astray. We need to watch out, as the disciples did, and remember that Jesus' promises are still true.

Think it through

1. What examples do you see today of people looking for signs to confirm God's promises? What is tempting about them?

2. What examples have you come across of detailed speculation about the future, and attempts to interpret Bible prophecies in terms of current world events? What do you think Jesus would say to them?

3. What did the disciples have to do to keep living for Jesus, despite the difficulties they faced?

4. If you live as a Christian, what difficulties will you face waiting for the future that Jesus promises?

5. What makes it worth enduring such difficulties?

6. What does Jesus say to our modern world about the future?

9

The hour has come

As Jesus and his disciples have moved towards Jerusalem, the tension has mounted. Many people hate him and want him killed. Moreover, Jesus himself has said that in Jerusalem he would be killed. When he arrives in Jerusalem, the tension increases further, for Jesus makes his opponents look foolish, which only makes them hate him all the more.

Now the sword that has been hanging over Jesus' head falls.

What will Jesus' followers do? Will they stand firm, as they insisted so many times they would? Will they heed the warning of chapter 13 and remain alert? Will the crowds who loved him take his side? Or will they disown Jesus for fear of the authorities? Will God intervene and somehow save his Messiah, or will the unthinkable happen?

As we read these two long and harrowing chapters, these questions are raised and answered. It is a story full of tension and drama, but Mark is not interested in merely telling a good story. As we watch what the people in the Gospel do, we are forced to ask: what will *we* do?

Others prepare for Jesus' death

Investigate

Read Mark 14:1-11.

1. What do the priests, the woman and Judas have in common?

2. What does Judas give the authorities that they have been looking for?

3. What do you think of Judas' action? Does the passage hint at his motives?

Jesus prepares for his death

Investigate

Read Mark 14:12-25.

1. What different reactions are there to Jesus' announcement that he will be betrayed?

2. Why is the betrayal particularly tragic?

The Passover

In Exodus 11-13, the Israelites were on the point of escaping from their slavery in Egypt. God had already sent terrible plagues on Egypt to persuade the Pharaoh to let them go free, but Pharaoh had consistently refused. Finally, God was going to send the last and most terrible judgement. Every first-born son in every household would be killed. The Israelites, however, were told to sacrifice a lamb and paint its blood on their doorposts. That way, the destroying angel would know which were God's people, and 'pass over' their houses. The people of Israel would be saved from God's judgement.

After that, the Israelites remembered their salvation each year by celebrating the Passover feast.

3. How does Jesus reinterpret this Passover meal?

4. If this is the new meaning of the Passover, what do you expect to happen to Jesus if he is the new Passover Lamb?

5. What is the significance of Jesus' promise in 14:25?

The hour has come!

Investigate

Read Mark 14:27-31.
1. What does Jesus predict will happen:

to him ?

to his followers?

2. What do you think of Peter's protestations? Are you positive or negative towards him?

Read Mark 14:32-42.
3. What is the struggle facing the disciples? How do you react to them?

4. What is the struggle facing Jesus? How do you react to him?

5. What does the arrival of Judas indicate?

Read Mark 14:43-52.

6. How do you end up feeling towards:

the disciples?

Judas?

Jesus?

Read Mark 14:53-72.

7. Why is it a surprise to find Peter still following Jesus?

8. At his trial, what is Jesus condemned for?

9. What does Jesus promise?

10. What does Peter's denial (in vv. 66-72) indicate:

about him?

about Jesus?

about Jesus' other promises?

The hour of judgement

Investigate

Read Mark 15:1-39.
1. Why was Jesus killed? What reasons can you find?

2. How do these reasons fit together?

3. How do you feel towards these characters and why?

Pilate

The crowd

The religious leaders

The disciples (they aren't even here!)

The gentile centurion (15:39)

4. Do you feel close to or distant from Jesus?

5. What is the effect of all this? What does the story make you want to do?

Our familiarity with the story of Jesus' death can blind us to what a shocking narrative it is. It is a heart-wrenching story, and we cannot help wondering why they would do this to Jesus. The way the story is told makes us feel repulsed at everyone who has betrayed or mistreated or abused Jesus. And yet, curiously, as the story proceeds we can also feel distant from Jesus himself, as if *we too* have deserted him on the cross.

This is the climax of the Gospel. These are the events the whole story has been leading towards, and which Jesus has predicted with increasing urgency since chapter 8. In these chapters, two of the main themes of Mark's Gospel come together. Firstly, Jesus is clearly crucified as the Messiah or 'King of Israel'. This is the charge the Sanhedrin finds him guilty of; this is the taunt the soldiers hurl at him; and this is the sign mockingly nailed above his head. Israel's king has come to his people; and yet they have rejected him and handed him over to the Gentiles to be killed.

Secondly, Jesus dies as the Suffering Servant who gives his life to save his people. Note the bitter irony of the taunts: "He saved others, but he can't save himself!" (v. 31). Jesus' enemies are unwittingly expressing the very heart of what is taking place. Jesus is in fact dying to save others, as a "ransom for many". He is drinking the cup of God's judgement, being forsaken by his Father, so that he could open up access to God for all his people (symbolised in the tearing of the temple curtain).

In yet another ironic touch, the crucifixion concludes with the confession of the pagan centurion. He alone of all those present recognizes what we the readers have known from the very beginning: that Jesus is the Son of God! And yet he does so as he witnesses how he died.

The challenge we are left with is: Will his response be our response?

Think it through

1. What makes Jesus attractive in these chapters?

2. Why did Jesus have to die?

3. What is the right response to Jesus' death? How do we receive the benefits of Jesus' death?

4. Have you taken advantage of Jesus' death?

10

He is not here

Will you join in our crusade?
Who will be strong and stand with me?
Somewhere beyond the barricade
Is there a world you long to see?

Songs like this one (from *Les Miserables*) express the human longing for a new and better world. We want justice, and peace, and a better place where suffering is no more.

However, according to Mark's Gospel, a new world *has* begun— God's new world. And for excitement and grandeur, nothing compares with it.

The end of Jesus?

Investigate

Read Mark 15:40-41.
1. Do you identify with the women? Explain your response.

2. What do they do?

Read Mark 15:42-46.
3. Do you identify with Joseph? Explain your response.

4. What have we, the readers, been waiting for that Joseph is also waiting for? (cf. 1:15; 4:26-29; 4:30-32; 9:1; 13:29; 14:25)

5. What happens to these expectations now that Jesus is buried?

Read Mark 16:1-8.
6. What is the significance of what the women find? Look up:

Mark 9:31

Mark 10:33-34

Mark 13:24-26 (cf. Dan 7:13-14)

Mark 14:62

7. If these expectations have now been fulfilled, what should happen next? Look back over:

Mark 9:9

Mark 13:26-27

Mark 14:9

Mark 1:16-18

Mark 14:28

8. What does happen? (v. 8)

9. Was the women's response right or wrong? Do you feel like condemning or rebuking them? Explain your response.

10. What is the effect of this last verse in Mark?

Just the beginning

"He has risen! He is not here", the man dressed in white says. And then we know that the expectations and predictions have all come true. The Son of Man has risen after his fiery ordeal (remember 10:33-34). He has come to the Ancient of Days (remember 13:24-26), and is now seated at the right hand of God (remember 14:62). Jesus' enemies have been shown to be wrong!

The man in white instructs the women to tell Jesus' disciples to meet him in Galilee as predicted (14:28). Now the resurrection has happened, it is a time for telling people what was previously kept secret (9:9), a time for taking the gospel to the world (13:10, 14:9), a time for the elect to be gathered (13:27), a time for the disciples to start their fishing for people (1:16-20), a time for the gospel of Jesus Christ the Son of God to be proclaimed. Mark's story has led up to this moment: but it is not the end, it is just the beginning.

What do we think of the women? With this great command to speak the good news of Jesus, the point to which the whole story has been leading up to, they are silent! Their silence is wrong, of course, but we sympathise. We, too, know the experience of fear, especially when we know we should speak up for Christ and his gospel. Yet silence is wrong, because after the resurrection is a time for gospel proclaiming. The moving dilemma faced by the women challenges us to think about our own silence. Even if we're afraid, it is still time to speak, because there is an empty tomb, Christ has risen, the kingdom of God has arrived!

In God's plan for this world there is only one event left to come. Jesus will return to share the kingdom of God with his people. The time between his resurrection and his return is a time for the gospel to be proclaimed, so that people from all nations can be invited to enter the kingdom of God now, before it is too late. This gospel is still being proclaimed, some 30 lifetimes later. Mark has told us where it all began: it began with Jesus Christ, the Son of God. He came with a mission. His mission continues: will you join him in his mission?

Think it through

1. What are the consequences of following Jesus in this modern world?

2. What costs?

3. What benefits?

4. If all that Mark says is true, how does it change:

   our dreams for the future of the world?

   our hopes and ambitions for our own future?

   our whole view of the world and what life is about?

Tips for leaders

Studying Mark

The studies in *News of the Hour,* like all of the Interactive and Topical Bible Studies from Matthias Media, are aimed to fall somewhere between a sermon and a set of unadorned discussion questions. The idea is to provide a little more direction and information than you would normally see in a set of printed Bible studies, but to maintain an emphasis on personal investigation, thought, discovery and application. We aim to give input and help, without doing all the work for the reader/studier.

Studying a Gospel, like Mark, presents particular problems for the small group leader. Not only are the passages longer than we might be used to studying (compared with, say, one of Paul's letters), but the way the Gospels communicate their message is a little different as well. They are narratives, and use the techniques of storytelling to make their point. They need to be read and studied with this in mind.

In practice, this will mean paying very careful attention to how the different episodes lead into each other, how themes or incidents from early in the story pop up again later on, how the different characters in the story relate to each other and are contrasted, how the physical action of the characters gives structure to the story (such as the three sea crossings in Mark), whether markers of time and place are important, and so on.

We have tried to model this approach in the studies, but it may still go against the grain for members in your group. As the leader, you will need to guard against the instinct to take the familiar stories out of context, or to treat them as separate entities each with their own 'moral'. Another common tendency is to read theology from elsewhere in the Bible (especially in the Epistles) back into the Gospel stories. It is not as if Mark will contain a *different* theology, but we do need to let the book speak for itself, with its own particular concerns and emphases.

In terms of commentaries that might be of assistance in your preparation, we would recommend the following:

The Gospel of Mark, by William L. Lane, (New International Commentary on the New Testament; Eerdmans)

The Servant King—Reading Mark Today, by Paul Barnett (Aquila Press)

Like all our studies, these are designed to work in a group on the assumption that the group members have worked through the material in advance. If this is not happening in your group it will obviously change the way you lead the study.

If the group is preparing...

If all is well, and the group is well-prepared, then reading through *all* the text, and answering *all* the questions will be time consuming and probably quite boring. It is not designed to work this way in a group.

The leader needs to go through the study thoroughly in advance and work out how to lead a group discussion using the text and questions as a *basis*. You should be able to follow the order of the study through pretty much as it is written. But you will need to work out which things you are going to omit, which you are going to glide over quite quickly, and which you are going to concentrate on and perhaps add supplementary discussion questions too.

Obviously, as with all studies, this process of selection and augmentation will be based on what your *aims* are for this study for your particular group. You need to work out where you want to get to as a main emphasis, teaching point or application point at the end. The material itself will certainly head you in a certain direction, but there will usually be various emphases you can bring out, and a variety of applications to think about.

The slabs of text in each study need to be treated as a resource for discussion, not something to be simply read out. This will mean highlighting portions to talk about, adding supplementary discussion questions and ideas to provoke discussion where you think that would be helpful for your particular group, and so on.

The same is true for the 'Investigate' and 'Think it through' questions. You need to be selective, according to where you want the whole thing to go. Some questions you will want to do fairly quickly or omit altogether. Others you will want to concentrate on—because they are difficult or because they are crucial or both— and in these cases you may want to add a few questions of your own if you think it would help.

You may also need to add some probing questions of your own if your group is giving too many 'pat' answers, or just reproducing the ideas in the text sections without actually grappling with the biblical text for themselves.

There is room for flexibility. Some groups, for example, read the text and do the 'Investigate' questions in advance, but save the 'Think it through' questions for the group discussion.

If the group isn't preparing...

This obviously makes the whole thing a lot harder (as with any study). Most of the above still applies. But if your group is not doing much preparation, your role is even more crucial and active. You will have to be even more careful in your selection and emphasis, and in asking supplementary questions—you will have to convey the basic content, as well as develop it in the direction of personal application. Reading through the *whole* study in the group will still be hard going. In your selection, you will probably need to read more sections of text together (selecting the important bits), and will not be able to glide over comprehension questions so easily.

If the group is not preparing, it does make it harder—not impossible, but a good reason for encouraging your group to do at least some preparation.

Conclusion

No set of printed studies can guarantee a good group learning experience. No book can take the place of a well-prepared thought-ful leader who knows where he or she wants to take the group, and guides them gently along that path.*

Our Bible studies aim to be a resource and handbook for that process. They will do a lot of the work for you. All the same, they need to be *used* not simply followed.

For further help in running your group, Matthias Media publishes a training course in small group leadership called *Growth Groups*; a training course on understanding the Bible, *Postcard from Palestine*; a bible overview. *Get into the Bible;* and a course on basic Christian doctrine, *The Blueprint*. Call us on 0845 225 0880 for a catalogue and further details.

Who are we?

Ever since 'St Matthias Press' first opened its doors in 1988, our aim has been to provide the Christian community with products of a uniformly high standard—both in their biblical faithfulness and in the quality of the writing and production.

Now known as The Good Book Company, we have grown to become an international provider of user-friendly resources, with Christians of all sorts using our Bible studies, books, Briefings, audio cassettes, videos and training courses.

Buy direct from us and save

If you order your resources direct from us, you not only save time and money, you invest in more great resources for the future:

- you save time—we usually despatch our orders the same day.
- you can save money—we give discounts for bulk orders of 10 or more.
- you help keep us afloat—because we get more from each sale, buying from us direct helps us to stay alive in the difficult world of publishing.

Please call us for a free catalogue of all our resources, including an up-to-date list of other titles in this Interactive Bible Studies series. Some details of IBS titles are contained on the following page.

| ☎ 0845 225 0880 | Elm House, 37 Elm Road, New Malden, Surrey KT3 3HB | FAX 0845 225 0990 (pay by credit card or invoice) |

Email: admin@thegoodbook.co.uk
www.thegoodbook.co.uk

Other Interactive and Topical Bible Studies from Matthias Media:

Our Interactive Bible Studies (IBS) and Topical Bible Studies (TBS) are a valuable resource to help you keep feeding from God's Word. The IBS series works through passages and books of the Bible; the TBS series pulls together the Bible's teaching on topics, such as money or prayer. As at January 2003, the series contains the following titles:

OLD TESTAMENT

FULL OF PROMISE
(THE BIG PICTURE OF THE O.T.)
Authors: Phil Campbell
& Bryson Smith, 8 studies

BEYOND EDEN (GENESIS 1-11)
Authors: Phillip Jensen
and Tony Payne, 9 studies

THE ONE AND ONLY
(DEUTERONOMY)
Author: Bryson Smith,
8 studies

**THE GOOD, THE BAD
& THE UGLY** (JUDGES)
Author: Mark Baddeley,
10 studies

FAMINE & FORTUNE (RUTH)
Authors: Barry Webb &
David Hohne, 4 studies

THE EYE OF THE STORM (JOB)
Author: Bryson Smith,
6 studies

THE SEARCH FOR MEANING
(ECCLESIASTES)
Author: Tim McMahon,
9 studies

TWO CITIES (ISAIAH)
Authors: Andrew Reid and
Karen Morris, 9 studies

KINGDOM OF DREAMS
(DANIEL)
Authors: Andrew Reid and
Karen Morris, 8 studies

WARNING SIGNS (JONAH)
Author: Andrew Reid, 6 studies

BURNING DESIRE
(OBADIAH & MALACHI)
Authors: Phillip Jensen and
Richard Pulley, 6 studies

NEW TESTAMENT

THE GOOD LIVING GUIDE
(MATTHEW 5:1-12)
Authors: Phillip Jensen
and Tony Payne, 9 studies

NEWS OF THE HOUR (MARK)
Author: Peter Bolt, 10 studies

FREE FOR ALL (GALATIANS)
Authors: Phillip Jensen
& Kel Richards, 8 studies

WALK THIS WAY (EPHESIANS)
Author: Bryson Smith,
8 studies

PARTNERS FOR LIFE
(PHILIPPIANS)
Author: Tim Thorburn,
8 studies

THE COMPLETE CHRISTIAN
(COLOSSIANS)
Authors: Phillip Jensen
and Tony Payne, 8 studies

ALL LIFE IS HERE (1 TIMOTHY)
Authors: Phillip Jensen
and Greg Clarke, 9 studies

RUN THE RACE (2 TIMOTHY)
Author: Bryson Smith,
6 studies

THE PATH TO GODLINESS
(TITUS)
Authors: Phillip Jensen and
Tony Payne, 6 studies

**FROM SHADOW TO
REALITY** (HEBREWS)
Author: Joshua Ng, 10 studies

THE IMPLANTED WORD (JAMES)
Authors: Phillip Jensen and
K.R. Birkett, 8 studies

HOMEWARD BOUND (1 PETER)
Authors: Phillip Jensen and
Tony Payne, 10 studies

ALL YOU NEED TO KNOW
(2 PETER)
Author: Bryson Smith,
6 studies

THE VISION STATEMENT
(REVELATION)
Author: Greg Clarke, 9 studies

TOPICAL BIBLE STUDIES

BOLD I APPROACH (PRAYER)
Author: Tony Payne,
6 studies

CASH VALUES (MONEY)
Author: Tony Payne,
5 studies

THE BLUEPRINT (DOCTRINE)
Authors: Phillip Jensen
& Tony Payne, 11 studies

WOMAN OF GOD
(THE BIBLE ON WOMEN)
Author: Terry Blowes, 8 studies